GRAPHIC LIBRARY™

INVENTIONS AND DISCOVERY

Johann Gutenberg —and the— Printing Press

by Kay Melchisedech Olson
illustrated by Tod Smith

Consultant:
Eric White, PhD
Curator of Special Collections
Bridwell Library, Southern Methodist University
Dallas, Texas

Capstone press®
Mankato, Minnesota

Graphic Library is published by Capstone Press,
151 Good Counsel Drive, P.O. Box 669, Mankato, Minnesota 56002.
www.capstonepress.com

1 2 3 4 5 6 11 10 09 08 07 06

Library of Congress Cataloging-in-Publication Data
Olson, Kay Melchisedech.
     Johann Gutenberg and the printing press/ by Kay Melchisedech Olson; illustrated by
Tod Smith.
     p. cm.—(Graphic library. Inventions and discovery)
     Includes bibliographical references and index.
     ISBN-13: 978-0-7368-6482-4 (hardcover)
     ISBN-10: 0-7368-6482-2 (hardcover)
     ISBN-13: 978-0-7368-7517-2 (softcover pbk.)
     ISBN-10: 0-7368-7517-4 (softcover pbk.)
     1. Gutenberg, Johann, 1397?–1468—Juvenile literature. 2. Printers—Germany—
Biography—Juvenile literature. 3. Printing—History—Origin and antecedents—Juvenile
literature. 4. Books—History—Juvenile literature. I. Smith, Tod, ill. II. Title. III. Series.
Z126.Z7O47 2007
686'.1092—dc22   2006008177

Summary: In graphic novel format, tells the story of Johann Gutenberg and the invention
     of the printing press.

Designers
Jason Knudson and Juliette Peters

Colorist
Brent Schoonover

Editor
Donald Lemke

Table of Contents

Chapter 1

Hand-Copied Books

During the 1400s, books were rare and valuable. In Mainz, Germany, each page of every book was hand-lettered by scribes.

Many scribes were monks who devoted their lives to the church. But demand for books was so great that many young men worked as scribes in scriptoriums at universities.

Our fastest scribes can finish several pages a day.

Who makes the colored decorations?

You must work many years to earn such an honor. Only the best are trusted with the colored ink.

Nicholas came to Mainz many times over the next few years. He and Gutenberg became close friends.

What have you been doing since we last met, Nicholas?

I have spent far too much time listening to arguments from churches around Germany.

What kind of arguments?

The Bible is the word of God, but scribes can make mistakes copying it. One scribe, copying a passage from Genesis, printed a "w" instead of a "t."

What harm could that cause?

The passage should have read, "On the seventh day you will not do any work."

But the passage read, "On the seventh day you will now do any work."

8

Chapter 2

A Secret Project

In early 1428, Gutenberg searched for a house to rent in Strasbourg, about 125 miles away from Mainz.

You and your cat would be quite comfortable here.

ROOM FOR RENT

What does one man and a cat need with a large place?

Very strange.

No, I require a much larger place with plenty of privacy.

Dunne, Heilman, and Dritzhen also provided money to fund the work. At the end of five years, the men would share whatever profits they had made.

You write out the terms of our contract and each of us will sign.

To keep our partnership secret, we must work separately. We should not be seen together or people may discover our plans.

While his three partners were busy working elsewhere, Gutenberg experimented with ink and paper.

The linseed oil, soot, and amber must be mixed in exactly the right amount. The paper must be soft enough to accept the ink.

But paper that is too soft will make the ink run. The letters then are not sharp and clear.

13

The Printing Business

Fust now owned Gutenberg's life work. But the Bibles were not quite finished, and Fust knew nothing of the art of printing.

Peter, I need you to finish the job on these Bibles.

You took me in and adopted me. You educated me and helped me get work. How can I refuse?

As Gutenberg had predicted, the printed Bibles made a great deal of money. Fust and his adopted son were very wealthy and continued in the printing business.

I had this special symbol made for us. It will symbolize an original printing by Fust and Schoeffer.

The world will see our mark and recognize our greatness.

Although he was alone and unrecognized for his achievement with printing the Bible, Gutenberg saw what his art had started.

The demand for printed books continued to grow.

Gutenberg managed to complete other printing projects in his lifetime. He was extremely careful about details, so his progress was often slow.

Rejectus ta tu in mūdo mūas
Reijcio ex re et iaco as coponi
ci reiectū reijcere.1.itey ul retro i
iectus ta tū.et reiecto tas fre.Et
duo J.cōponitur enim ex re et i
a in J.De hoc dixi in iacio iacis
Reiuuenesco as inchoatiuū a r
Relacō onis.a refero refers d2.

But his work was always beautiful.

The Archbishop of Mainz died in 1459. His replacement, angry with all who opposed him, forced most of the young men of Mainz to leave town. Many were printers, who took their skill to other cities in Europe.

Don't worry, my friend. I am too old to leave. The archbishop will allow me to remain in Mainz for the little time I have left on earth.

By the 1460s, German print shops opened in Venice and Rome. Within 10 years, Italy became the major center of book printing in Europe.

JOHANN SPEYER PRINTER

JOHANN SPEYER PRINTER

In 1468, Gutenberg died. He was buried at the Franciscan monastery in Mainz. Few people noticed his passing.

JOHANN GUTENBERG

In the 1470s, an Englishman named William Caxton printed books for literature and science rather than religion. Soon, books became popular among a very wide range of people.

In the 1700s and 1800s, printing was a major industry in North America and Europe. Printers like Benjamin Franklin used the same technology invented by Gutenberg hundreds of years earlier.

Gutenberg was never recognized for his invention in his own lifetime.

Today, Gutenberg is known as the man who created one of the greatest inventions of all time—printing with moveable type.

27

Johann Gutenberg
and the Printing Press

Little is known about Johann Gutenberg. He was born in Mainz, Germany, around 1397, but no one knows the exact date. Gutenberg's father was named Friele and his mother was Else. Johann grew up with his parents, one brother, and one sister.

Nicholas of Cusa was born in 1401 and was about three years younger than Gutenberg. Nicholas became a lawyer and important church leader. In February 1432, Nicholas was sent to Mainz on business. It is possible that he and Gutenberg met at that time, but no one knows for sure.

The genius of Gutenberg's art was the metal type he made. Each letter was exactly the same height as all the others, so the printing would be even. Blank pieces were made to fit between words. Each line of type fit exactly into the form. Gutenberg was very particular and insisted that each page be absolutely perfect.

Gutenberg kept his metal letters in drawers called cases. Each case had dividers to keep all the different letters separate. He kept the capital letters in the upper case and small letters in the lower case. Even today, capital letters are known as "uppercase" letters and small letters are called "lowercase" letters.

When he started printing the pages of the Bible, Gutenberg had two columns of print on each page with 40 lines in each column. As his costs grew, Gutenberg decided to save on paper by putting 42 lines in each column. He printed the rest of the Bible pages with two columns of 42 lines each. Original Gutenberg Bibles are known as the 42-line Bible, even though some pages have columns with only 40 lines.

Of the nearly 200 Bibles Gutenberg printed, only 48 still exist today. But recent technology has made it easier than ever for anyone to view this priceless book. Digital copies are now available, allowing the general public to see all 1,282 pages on their computers.

Glossary

engrave (en-GRAYV)—to cut a design or letters into a metal, wood, or glass surface

monastery (MON-uh-ster-ee)—a group of buildings where monks live and work

novice (NOV-iss)—someone who joins a religious order for a trial period before taking vows

scribe (SKRIBE)—a person who copies books, letters, contracts, and other documents by hand

scriptorium (skrip-TOR-ee-uhm)—a copying room for scribes

vellum (VEL-uhm)—fine parchment paper made from the skin of a calf, lamb, or baby goat

Internet Sites

FactHound offers a safe, fun way to find Internet sites related to this book. All of the sites on FactHound have been researched by our staff.

Here's how:
1. Visit *www.facthound.com*
2. Choose your grade level.
3. Type in this book ID **0736864822** for age-appropriate sites. You may also browse subjects by clicking on letters, or by clicking on pictures and words.
4. Click on the **Fetch It** button.

FactHound will fetch the best sites for you!

Read More

Koscielniak, Bruce. *Johann Gutenberg and the Amazing Printing Press.* Boston: Houghton Mifflin, 2003.

Pollard, Michael. *Johann Gutenberg: Master of Modern Printing.* Giants of Science. Woodbridge, Conn.: Blackbirch Press, 2001.

Rees, Fran. *Johannes Gutenberg: Inventor of the Printing Press.* Signature Lives. Minneapolis: Compass Point Books, 2006.

Bibliography

Gutenberg Homepage. http://www.gutenberg.de/english/

Ing, Janet Thompson. *Johann Gutenberg and His Bible: A Historical Study.* New York: Typophiles, 1988.

Kapr, Albert. *Johann Gutenberg: The Man and His Invention.* Aldershot, England; Brookfield, Vt.: Scolar Press, 1996.

Man, John. *Gutenberg: How One Man Remade the World with Words.* New York: John Wiley & Sons, 2002.

University of Texas at Austin. *Gutenberg Bible at the Ransom Center.* Harry Ransom Center Online Exibition http://www.hrc.utexas.edu/exhibitions/permanent/gutenberg/

Index